ALL OUR RELATIONS

All Our Relations

GreenSpirit connections with the more-than-human world

Edited by
Marian Van Eyk McCain

With contributions by
David Abram, Clea Danaan, Franziska Holmes,
Kathleen Martin, Sky McCain, Susan Meeker-Lowry,
Helen Moore, Eleanor O'Hanlon, Rupert Sheldrake,
Stephanie Sorrell, Suzannah Stacey
and Hilary Wilmshurst

Published by GreenSpirit
137 Ham Park Road, London E7 9LE
www.greenspirit.org.uk

Registered Charity No. 1045532

ISBN 978-0-9935983-4-0

Design and artwork by Stephen Wollaston (Santoshan)
Printed by CreateSpace and Amazon

Front cover image © Ducu59us/Shutterstock.com
Page 11 and 12 photo © Soru Epotok/Shutterstock.com
Page 43 and 44 photo © Utopia_88/Shutterstock.com
Page 69 and 70 photo © Serif Image Collection 3
Page 91 and 92 photo © Eric Isselee/Shutterstock.com
Page 105 and 106 photo: © Vanessa Clark

CONTENTS

INTRODUCTION

All in the Same Boat

H ave you noticed how, even though we know the story of evolution, many of the ways that we talk about Nature and about our fellow creatures serve to drive a semantic wedge between 'it' and us, between 'them' and us? So much so, in fact, that it is quite a challenge to talk about other life forms without falling into the trap of separating ourselves from them with our words.

As we all know, there is absolutely no doubt whatsoever that our species Homo sapiens is a member of the Kingdom called Animalia. In other words, we are animals. Like all other members of that Kingdom, we have a slot into which we fit. You can find our particular slot on any diagram of the Animalia tree. Specifically, we belong to the Phylum: Chordata (we have spines), the Subphylum: Vertebrata (a special sort of spines), the Class: Mammalia (we suckle our young), the Order: Primates (along with apes, and monkeys), the Family: Hominidae (one of the so-called 'great apes') and the Genus: Homo (men and women, boys and girls).

So yes, we are definitely animals. Yet from the way we often speak about ourselves—and even the way we think about ourselves—you might come to the conclusion that we, in our culture, are in some sort of denial about it.

The problem is that after centuries of imagining ourselves as separate from the rest of the animal kingdom and forgetting that all of these other life forms are related to us by our very DNA, our language has in turn been shaped to a huge extent by our beliefs. So that makes it hard to avoid the linguistic traps.

For example we find ourselves using phrases like 'humans and animals,' as though we were something different and not animals. We find ourselves talking about how much we enjoy 'walking in Nature,' as though there were any place on our planet were Nature isn't. Because of course Nature is us. Nature is in us and everywhere and in everything. Even in the heart of the city, Nature is not just the pigeons and rats and cockroaches and mice and the slivers of living green that grow up in the cracks between the paving stones, but all-pervasive. The air is full of unseen creatures; our own bodies have other creatures living on and within them, creatures in their millions, most of them smaller that can be seen with the naked eye, all living and breathing and doing their thing.

We find ourselves falling into these linguistic traps, not just out of habit but because it can be hard to find other, better alternatives. However, just as wheels create ruts and ruts in turn capture wheels, not only does thought shape language but language ends up shaping thought and perpetuating attitudes. It takes a big effort to heave ourselves out of the rut and pay conscious, mindful attention to the way we speak of other creatures.

The more we learn to stay mindful of this fact that we, too, are animals, the more offensive it can start sounding to our ears when we hear others use the word 'animal' pejoratively, as in 'He's no better than an animal,' (particularly when we reflect on the irony of it, given that we ourselves are the species with the very worst behaviour record of all time!) Yet hopefully, the more we stay mindful, the better we shall become at developing a vocabulary that better reflects the true relationships between ourselves and what author David Abram calls the 'more-than-human' world.

The very first time I learned that in the Native American culture other species are referred to as 'all our relations,' I immediately felt the sheer 'rightness' of that term. Which is why I have chosen that phrase as the title for this little volume in the GreenSpirit book series: a book that that specifically honours all those other life forms with whom we share the planet.

They are all our relations. How we treat them, how we perceive them and feel about them and interact with them— and the extent to which we respect them—is, I maintain, a measure of our true humanity and a measure of our true worth. For along with them we make up the delicate web of life that makes this place liveable and beautiful. Whatever damage we do to that web, we do to ourselves, to each other, to our children and grandchildren and to all our relations of every size and kind. If they fail to thrive and survive, so do we. We are all in this together. All in the same small, fragile boat we call Planet Earth, floating in the dark, starry vastness of inhospitable space.

It is my pleasure and privilege to bring to you this collection of writings that honours, in many difference ways and voices, our GreenSpirit connections with all those members of the more-than-human world who travel alongside us in this little boat.

—Marian Van Eyk McCain

*   *   *

PART ONE

ENCOUNTERS

TODAY, OF ALL DAYS

In memory of Annette Tolson

Today a Hare leaps from the shadows of a thicket;
I'm its silent, motionless observer,
its ear-erect alertness, its wide eyeball watch.

Today shafts of Winter sunlight rouse me—
hair-tips stretching up to bathe
in its pale, ultra-violet tint.

Today the Oak's roots support me;
through its cleft and curvy leaves I breathe,
knotted arms crowning my dependence.

Today a crew of Rooks fly up
from tree-tops in gregarious, airy lifting;
I'm their co-arising everywhere.

Today the wind blows from the North;
I stand by my door—sense how Spirit
lives inside this house of bone.

Today thousands of Mycelia connect me,
by sugared strands invisibly through the earth;
I fruit browny-white; deliquesce here, there, nowhere.

© *Helen Moore. From her ecopoetry collection 'Hedge Fund, And Other Living Margins,' Shearsman Books, 2012.*

MEETINGS WITH MAGIC

Susan Meeker-Lowry, editor of Gaian Voices
in conversation with David Abram, author of
Spell of the Sensuous and *Becoming Animal*

Susan: I've not lost the sensibility I had as a child of the world as a magical place full of alive beings just waiting to engage in relationship. The fact that most people today no longer have a sense of this aliveness is, I feel, what makes the extreme devastation of the Earth possible. This is not to say that trees and rocks feel, speak, see, hear as humans do. A tree is a tree. A rock is a rock. A spider is a spider. We are each very different creatures, all strands in the web of life...

David: You feel like you're actually in an interchange of sorts with an intelligence that is awake like your own but very, very different. Its shape, its organs, and tissues are different from ours, its engagement with the world is from an entirely different angle than ours. I think that epitomizes the experience we might call magic. But this notion of magic has been eclipsed in the last couple of centuries by religious notions that obscure the fact that there's nothing supernatural about magic, it's really something that grows out of the Earth itself.

Susan: What I love about your perspective and your writing is how you find the words to communicate that. It seems to me that you want to engage the reader in actually experiencing and feeling what they might if they were out there with you in the woods, for instance. You want people to feel it inside so that it becomes part of them, not just something they're reading or listening to.

David: Well one simple thing to say is that we in the over-civilized world are steeped in assumptions that juxtapose the body and the mind as two different things, that juxtapose spirit and matter as two different substances. So much of my work involves recognizing that mind or sentience is something that comes with having a body, of any form or shape, particularly one that needs to orient and navigate in the world, so it's going to need to think, decide, choose. That body and mind are not separable. Similarly matter is not something other than spirit—it's the very flesh of spirit. This latest book of mine is called *Becoming Animal*, because it's about what if we really were to identify with our animality and celebrate the fact that we're animals, extraordinary animals but animals nonetheless, and hence in many ways just one of the gang here. How would we speak of even the most ordinary aspects of our world that we take for granted and that we currently think of according to assumptions that are very otherworldly, that see the source of everything beyond this world? Can we think otherwise? Can we speak otherwise? I think so. But it could just as easily and perhaps maybe more appropriately be called Becoming Earth. I think we tap a tremendous reservoir of power and strength when we allow that we're entirely born of this breathing planet and that we really are nothing other than parts of Earth. That our real flesh is this immense spherical metabolism that envelopes us, that the deep, dense energy of the Earth is pulsing into us all the time. When we think of ourselves as not just earthly beings, but as Earth then we have all that wildness and all that power surging through us to meet whatever challenges come up. It doesn't make it easy by any means. But it alters the way we feel.

Susan: I remember when I was a little girl we were driving on a highway where workers were blasting huge granite cliffs to widen the road. And I looked at my father and said, "Well, that must really hurt the rocks." Everyone in the car looked at me like I was an idiot. But to me the idea of having something like that shoved into me to blast my body apart would be a painful thing. And it just made sense to me that the rock would hurt.

David: I wish more of us were able to tap into and remember those early childhood experiences where that kind of empathy was much closer to everyone. Today our adult selves quickly jump in and say, "Come on, a rock? It doesn't have senses, it's an entirely different kind of presence from a human being who has conscious awareness." But that itself is caught up in so many assumptions. When in fact we and the rock have a great deal in common. First and foremost the fact that we are material presences in the same Earth, that we are both shapes of matter, ways of being Earth. That's a huge kindredness that is entirely hidden by our contemporary assumption.

Susan: I get all of these different e-mail newsletters about issues that are of concern to me. And there was one that had a headline something like, "Study finds chickens have feelings." And I'm like, "Duh!"

David: But such is the goofy way we've learned to speak at a time when other animals, to say nothing of plants and the land itself, are often spoken of as a set of mechanisms. Other animals are to be understood, if we're being objective, as a complex set of mechanical operations. We've learned to speak of them in such detached terms in order to submit them to the clear light of the scientific gaze. I need to be very clear that nothing I've written anywhere means to disparage the sciences. I've learned the bulk of what I know from the natural sciences. But I'm very aware that the ways of speaking within the sciences tend to lean upon metaphors that turn the world into something that can be built, taken apart, put back together. And this is very practical for the purposes of a particular bit of research, as long as one then translates the results back into the language of respectful encounter with a being that is as mysterious and elegant and present in the world as we are. But that translation never seems to happen. And so many people grow up and are educated into a way of looking at the rest of Nature as though it was just a set of objects without feelings, without sensations.

Susan: I have a beautiful garden and I spend as much time as I can there. When I open the gate and walk in it's full of such amazing spirits and life forms, bees and worms, all of it.

And I talk to everyone, out loud. I have conversations with all of these wonderful beings. It feeds me. I honestly don't know what I would do if I was one of those people who didn't know that this is the way it is. I imagine my life would feel so empty. No wonder people shop all the time! If the only life that is possible for us to have a relationship with is another human being, or maybe a dog or cat, then that's a very depleted world.

David: It's so important that it be out loud, yes! It would be a very depleted, impoverished world, and lonely as hell. And it's probably really bad for our immune systems to be cut off from the nourishment that comes from carrying on active relationships with everything. That doesn't mean that this world of multiple relationships is harmonious or purely sweet. It's filled with jagged edges and shadows and predation. And yet it's just really beautiful and nourishing. It's wild.

*   *   *

Editor's Note

These are extracts taken from a much longer interview published in *Gaian Voices*. My grateful thanks to Susan for allowing me to reprint them here.

WHALE

Eleanor O'Hanlon

Extracted, with permission, from her book
'Eyes of the Wild'

The gray whales come to us.

"*Tenemos amigos*," the boat driver Cuco Fisher says. "We have friends."

He cuts the outboard engine as the two whales swim towards our small open boat, their smoothly powerful undulations rising and falling through the lagoon's clear green water: a gray whale mother with her young calf by her side.

The whales surface alongside, an eruption of life from the deep, the water rippling in shining falls from their backs as the mother exhales, a gust of warm spray that briefly hangs in a mist plume on the air. The calf lifts its head above the water and I glimpse the ancient, undersea face—the dimples on the dark skin of the upper jaw, each one with a single bristle of short hair; the long mouth with gently rounded lips, the top lip slightly overlapping. Then the calf sinks onto the strong support of the mother's back and the pair submerges, becoming little more than vague suggestions of enormous presence until they disappear into the green depths.

In the silence they leave behind, I wait, gazing into the water in the hope they will surface again.

Slowly, surely, with silken gliding, the mother returns to

the surface. There is no stir, no ripple through the water as she rises, only the massive darkening of her body, coming more clearly into focus until she breaks through the surface beside me, and her blowholes pulse again with that same great whoosh of exhaled air.

The plosive power of the whale mother's breathing resounds with the expansive dimensions of her life. Her body extends forty feet or more beneath the water—twice the length of our open boat. The double curve of her tail flukes spreads around twelve feet wide. She weighs perhaps thirty tons, and the mottled white patches on her dark-gray skin, the absence of a dorsal fin, and the colonies of barnacles that cluster roughly on her back and sides distinguish her as one of the gray whales of the Eastern Pacific, also known as the California Gray, *Eschrichtius robustus*.

Each year the gray whales make one of the longest and most arduous journeys of any creature on Earth as they swim between their principal summer feeding grounds in the Bering Strait and the southern Chukchi Sea and the sheltered lagoons along the Pacific coast of Baja California where they mate and give birth between January and April. San Ignacio is the only one of the lagoons that has not been affected by development. It is set within the Vizcaino Biosphere Reserve, a UNESCO World Heritage site and the largest nature reserve in Mexico.

When this gray whale mother knew she was pregnant, she left Baja California and turned north, swimming an average of eighty miles each day and following the entire Pacific coast of North America within a few miles of shore until she reached the Bering Sea and Strait. Although she may have foraged along the way, the richly productive Arctic waters are where she was able to feed most intensively. In late autumn she began her journey south, to bring her calf safely to birth inside the lagoon's mangrove channels, where the sheltered waters helped her raise it to the surface for its first breath.

After twelve months curled inside its mother's womb, the newborn whale calf's first movements in the water are wobbly and uncertain. The mother rolls onto her back to hold her baby against her chest and strokes it gently with her flippers. When the calf has grown stronger on the extraordinary richness of her milk—gray whale milk is more than 50% fat and contains three times as much protein as human milk—she leads it to more challenging waters near the lagoon exit, to swim through the powerful currents and develop the stamina and coordination it will need to follow her north.

In the past year alone, this gray whale mother has swum perhaps 10,000 miles or more while carrying her calf within her body. She will feed it, teach it, love and protect it with unstinting, implacable devotion as they make their epic journey north together. By the time they both arrive in the Bering Strait, the mother will have been largely fasting for eight months and she may have lost a third of her body weight.

With the mother alongside, the whale calf raises its head above the surface—as curious, playful and eager for attention as any young mammal—and I splash it on the nose with handfuls of water, a sensation which it clearly enjoys.

Then the mother does something utterly extraordinary. She sinks beneath her calf and deliberately brings it closer to the surface by supporting it on her back, so that I can touch it easily on the head and nose. As I run my hands along the calf's lips, the mouth opens with an audible release of suction and my fingers brush the baleen fibers that line the upper jaw in place of teeth among the grays and all other baleen whales.

No wild creature can make a greater gesture of trust than to bring you her newborn and allow you to touch it. This mother is bringing me what is most precious to her, the calf she has carried for twelve months in her body and brought to birth a few weeks ago in this lagoon. The next time she surfaces, she lingers alongside and I begin speaking aloud to her, naturally and without thinking. I tell her how beautiful she is, how happy I am to meet her. She blows again, a short misty burst like a snort, and submerges. A moment later the wooden *panga* is rattled by the power of her more forceful underwater exhalation. It rises out of the water, rocks and settles back, and I realize with shock that she has just lifted us up on her back and placed us gently down again.

Mother and calf flow over and under and around each other; they circle the boat in long graceful turns, sink and rise again with the water sparkling on their wet sides like stars. At times the mother turns through the water in a slow, powerful rotation that takes her from her belly to her back. Again, the boat rocks as she pushes it with her head from below. Yet I never have a moment's fear of her great size and power. She moves with completely refined, sensitive awareness through the whole of her body.

When the mother surfaces next, she comes close enough for me to reach out and touch her. I run my hands along the skin of her side, which feels indescribably smooth, as though the texture has been endlessly refined by the washing of the sea. Her flesh is firm and cool beneath my hands. Through the physical contact with her body, a sense of the expansive dimensions of her being opens inside me like soundings from some vast interior sea. As the depth of the meeting grows, it becomes an opening through which something entirely new keeps pouring—a wordless sense of connection with a greater life.

Turning onto one side, the whale gazes up at me through the water; looking down into her dark eye, ringed with folds of skin, I meet the lucid and tranquil gaze of an ancestor, one of the ancient ones of the Earth. I feel her taking me out, far out, of thought and linear time, beyond the limited concerns of my ordinary mind, into a profound sense of meeting with another being, whose consciousness is not separate from my own.

When she surfaces next with her calf by her side, the whale mother places her nose directly against the side of the panga and becomes completely still. Her blowholes are closed; her immense power is utterly composed and quiet. I reach out and touch her on the head with my right hand, then I put my left hand on her calf and join with them both on the undivided sea.

That evening, back at our camp on the lagoon shore, I try to write down something of the power of what I have experienced with the whale mother and her calf. But all that comes to me are a few terse words: *what was, on the day of creation, is, now.*

Eden, I think, is not simply a mythical place, or a metaphor for original innocence, or an outworn and divisive religious symbol. Eden is a state of being, and we are free to return every time we know ourselves again in deep communion with the rest of life.

*   *   *

MY ARGUMENT WITH JAMILAH

Marian Van Eyk McCain

"Hey Jamilah," I said, "Look! Isn't he beautiful?"

She put down her cereal spoon and turned her head towards the window, following my gaze. Her coal-dark eyes opened wide. "Oh he is gorgeous!"

"He's called a superb blue wren," I said. "The male gets this amazing blue plumage in the Spring and—"

"I prefer not to know the names of birds," she said, pursing her lips slightly.

I looked at her in surprise.

"Why ever not?"

"For me, knowing their names spoils it," she said.

I didn't argue with her. Not outwardly anyway. She was a guest in our house. And she was helping us with our building project. I was hoping she and her partner would stay on and become part of our little retreat community in the foothills of the Australian Alps. So I didn't want to offend her.

Inside, though, I could feel myself composing my argument.

"But Jamilah," my argument went, "You need to know their names. It is human nature to want to know the names of things. Babies point and grunt and strain towards that knowing. Without it, we are wild, unincorporated creatures. Like the young Helen Keller before that epiphanal moment at the pump, when Annie Sullivan tapped out the word 'water' into her hand and suddenly she understood how to name— and therefore know—a world she could neither see nor hear."

"For me, knowing their names spoils it." That strange, bald statement kept rattling around in my mind.

"You see, Jamilah," I wanted to say, "Without a name, that little bird pecking on the window is just the reflection of light on feathers, a sensation, a moment in the landscape around your breakfast. A moment you may well forget. To me he is so much more. He has an identity. And therefore he has a yesterday, a tomorrow, a story, a personality and these all go together with his name.

"I want to tell you why he's pecking on the window. It's because he can see a rival in the windowpane, and has to vanquish him. He will peck that windowpane on and on, from now till lunchtime. Then he'll take a lunch break. And then, because he is a valiant warrior, this afternoon he'll come back and peck some more. And if the sun shines again tomorrow and that phantom rival appears in the glass again, he'll be back, obliged by his wrenny honour to peck and peck until the light goes or until instinct tells him it is time to stop, whichever happens first. He's called a "superb blue wren," Jamilah. That is who he is. He heads a family of several female wrens and some juveniles (none of whose colours blaze like his). And there will be a nest. Last year, it was in the lower branches of a silver wattle (*acacia dealbata*) and the brown snake (*Pseudonaja*) ate the eggs.

26

How could she not want to know the names? The thought continued to disturb me.

"Jamilah, I know it is wonderful and very spiritual to live in the moment. And I know you are not interested in the story of this bird. But without a name, without a story, this bird is like part of a stage set. Flat. Two-dimensional. A generic 'bird.' I have such difficulty with generic birds, you see. They frustrate me. I remember that day in transit at Honolulu airport when I walked down into the little garden they have there, and there were birds I could not name, flitting around in trees I could not name. One doesn't think of taking a bird guide in one's hand luggage in case one might need it in the transit lounge. But oh how I wished for one then. Maybe we bird-watching enthusiasts ('twitchers' we are called in England) are genetically different or something."

That was not a convincing argument, and I knew it.

How about...

"Well, Jamilah, it is probably because I am a writer that I have such a need to know their names. Words are so important to me, you see. Names carry so much. The word 'chickadee' hangs upside down on the page, head cocked, bright eyes looking at me. The word 'heron' stands all day in the margin, tall and still. The word 'swift' carves a sudden, swooping arc across the top of the page and is gone, leaving just a shrill, high note on the paper. The word 'partridge' lies low, between the other words, flattening itself against the paper, until I stumble over it and it flies off the page altogether with a sudden whirr of wings that takes me by surprise."

I think of Jamilah's dark eyes, and the way she looks at me.

She seems very confident. But I know there are chinks in her argument.

"Yet in many other ways, Jamilah, I know that words and names mean a lot to you. Although you profess to be an atheist, I recall how thrilled you were when you discovered that I knew how to say "There is no god but Allah and Mohammed is his prophet" in Arabic, and you wrote it for me in that elegant, curling script."

In my imagination, she is shaking her head.

"Oh Jamilah, it is probably because you have been so dominated by your thinking mind. It must have been hard for you, growing up female in your Middle Eastern culture, with parents who really wanted a boy instead of yet another girl. And being the only female in your year to get a Ph.D. in civil engineering. And it must be hard teaching those students of yours all day. I can see why you must long to switch off that thinking part of yourself and simply bask in the wordless, nameless joy of watching that pert little bird on the windowsill, with the sun shining on his bright, blue feathers."

Maybe that's true. But what about me? What am I defending? Why am I so keen for her to agree with me?

Jamilah, I haven't told you this, but one day, when I was a little girl, my grandmother, who was embroidering a tablecloth, sent me off with my butterfly net to capture some butterflies. She said there were going to be butterflies in the embroidery and she wanted to make sure she got the colours right. Delighted to be helpful, I spent hours hunting down a tortoiseshell, a red admiral, a brimstone and several others, bringing each one back triumphantly to show her.

She praised me. I was very happy. It was several years later, when I saw that finished tablecloth, with its generic, totally impossible butterflies, that the truth dawned on me. She had simply wanted to keep me occupied. I had brought her the butterflies. I had proudly told her their names. And now I felt foolish, dismayed and taken for a ride.

There is more. It is coming up from inside me now, from somewhere deeper than a childhood memory.

You know, Jamilah, I have never actually admitted this before, but there is part of me that wishes I could be more like you. I feel almost guilty that I want to attach all this thought, all this head stuff to this tiny bird, this tiny, feathered messenger from a world where nothing has a name and the present moment is all there is.

I am moving into new territory now.

Is there a way, Jamilah, that we humans, top-heavy with thoughts, opinions, ideas and concepts, laced into our worldviews and belief systems and identities as tightly as our great-grandmothers were laced into their corsets, could ever be as light and as fully present in the 'now' moment as that wren on the windowsill?

What if there were? What if we could be so free of all that baggage that we could truly meet each other, heart to heart, soul to soul? What if I could truly encounter another, whether a woman or man, an owl, a mouse, a mountain lion, or even a bug or a creosote bush, without the trappings of identity?

How important is identity anyway? Do you remember that song Suzanne Vega used to sing about playing with identities: "If I had met you on some journey...who would we be now?"

We can shape-shift so easily nowadays. Think of all those people in Internet chat rooms pretending to be professors and brain surgeons to impress the faceless others in cyberspace. It is a form of creativity, a kind of 21st Century adventuring...

But there is a deeper, bolder adventure than that. It is the adventure of shedding identity altogether. And perhaps—finally—learning to meet each other. Really meet. As we truly are, in our essence. To give the gift of ourselves, unpackaged.

I am getting old, Jamilah. I am closer to eighty than seventy now. When you and I sat together at breakfast, watching that wren at the window, I was still in my early fifties. Back then, I was clutching my favourite pieces of identity around me like a cloak, to keep out the chill of unknowing: mother, psychologist, therapist, author...

But now? Now, Jamilah, it is starting to feel different.

Have you heard of the Indian sage Ramana Maharshi? The spiritual practice he taught was a very simple one. Ask yourself: "Who am I?" Answer the question. Ask it again. And again, and again, and again. Keep on asking and answering until every possible answer has been exhausted. Only then—and it will probably take a whole lifetime—will you become enlightened.

Am I getting enlightened do you suppose, Jamilah? Or am I just a slightly dotty old woman, reminiscing about the past? Perhaps I am both, and more besides. Or perhaps I am none of those but simply a dust mote in a sunbeam, a ripple in the ocean, a movement in the shifting, swirling, changing dance of energy which is life on Earth.

I have not seen Jamilah for many years now. But the last time I saw her, she told me how much she enjoyed the months she spent in that retreat centre we were building in the mountains of Australia. She spoke of all the things she remembered. Above all, she has never forgotten the shining, blue visitor who pecked on the window at breakfast time. The one which, for her, had no name and never will.

*　　*　　*

DANCING WITH TREES

Kathleen Martin

E very time I pass the oak tree on our corner, I just know it's asking me to dance. I've had this kind of relationship with trees for as long as I can remember.

When I was too young to go to school but old enough to play in the backyard by myself, I remember grabbing the lower limbs of trees and hoisting myself up so that I could hang head down with my legs clamped tightly around a branch. I loved the upside down world that I saw. Maybe that's why I've always tended to look at things from a bit of a different perspective.

Throughout my childhood my fascination with trees continued. I built tree house after tree house with my friends. They just keep getting bigger and more complex as we advanced to taller and taller trees. The huge pine trees in the nearby woods also provided us with boats. We would jimmy large pieces of bark from the tree trunks and then use our pocketknives to whittle craft that we would sail down streams and across ponds. I got really good at making pine bark boats.

With the arrival of November would come pecan season. We would climb as high as we could in the pecan trees and then begin to sway back and forth. The pecans would shake loose and then we would shimmy down to gather as many pecans as we could in our pockets. I learned how to hold two pecans together in my one hand and then squeeze as hard as I could with both hands until they cracked. Pecans are best when you crack them yourself.

I remember learning the names of every kind of tree that I could find. I was fascinated by the different shapes of their leaves and loved to make crayon rubbings that I would keep under my bed and look at when it was too dark to see the trees. I really liked that some trees colored their own leaves when it got cold outside and then let them fall to the ground so that we could rake them into huge piles. We would jump into the piles, burying one another and scattering the leaves and then rake them into big piles again.

When I grew up and went to college, I lived in a dorm near a huge weeping willow tree. I fell in love with that tree. Its curtains of drooping branches fell all the way to the ground and offered me a perfect hideaway. Dorm life was difficult for me, but the shelter beneath my willow provided the privacy and quiet I so desperately needed. Then one day my willow tree was gone. It had been cut down and the ground around it was strewn with its remains. I'll never forget the horror and sense of loss that I felt with the death of my tree. I learned within time that I had hideaways within myself, places where I could find peace and solace. I would always be able to imagine my weeping willow.

I eventually married and my husband and I moved into a second story apartment with large windows surrounded by trees. We called it our tree house home. Later we had two small sons and lived in a one-story house. There was a huge cottonwood tree in our backyard. My husband built a very large tree house for our sons, but it was really for me. I used to go up there in the evenings after the boys were in bed, lie on my back and watch the stars through the tree limbs. Somehow the stars seem more reachable when you look at them through tree limbs.

Trees decided my last career move. I had two job offers. One was a lot better money-wise than the other. But the trees in the Pacific Northwest were the largest and most beautiful that I had ever seen. They seemed to be competing with the mountains for which could reach higher. I loved the way they stretched skyward and wept with each rain. We chose to live among those trees. Even though we have since moved to a place without large trees, I can close my eyes and still see those towering evergreens. I always will.

I have become a driftwood sculptor and gourd artist. I love the touch of wood and the satisfaction that comes with making its beauty visible to others. Wood surrounds me. To reach for it is one of the most natural acts in my world. So why would that oak tree on our corner not want to dance with me?

*   *   *

THE FLAME ROBIN

Sky McCain
Extracted, with permission from his book
'Planet as Self: An Earthen Spirituality'

There is just an indirect hint of dusk since the sun lowered itself behind the hill over an hour ago. As I look out over the small valley stretched out below me a soft murmur of a strong but gentle wind draws my eyes expectantly up and to my right along the distant eucalyptus-lined hillside. Very soon, along the ridge, leaves begin to tumble and quake until, like a wave approaching the shore, a sighing, invisible column of air makes its way along and down through the gully, ruffling leaves and becoming louder as it moves. And then all is quiet and still again. I can't explain why this scene, this momentary passage of breeze through one little gully holds so much fascination for me. I know there is a message there from Gaia, but I lack the ability to comprehend it.

I cross my legs and resume my idle gaze out along the valley before me. Suddenly, a flame robin alights on the toe of my boot. The Australian flame robin exhibits the same qualities of stillness and stealth as flycatchers do: that same intent peering ahead for prey. Watching these little birds is one of my favorite pastimes. I have often noticed that no sooner do I pound in another garden stake and walk away than ... zoom! a robin alights on it. But to have this beautiful little being choose my upturned boot as a perch nearly stops my heart. I realize I am holding my breath. The pleasure of being so near and in a strange way intimate with a wild creature of the air invokes a feeling of privilege. I feel honoured by such a presence. Soon, the robin flies down to peck at something and then on to a garden fence post. Of course, to the robin, I am just another elevated stick. So the pleasure is all mine.

*   *   *

WOLF

Eleanor O'Hanlon
Extracted, with permission, from her book
'Eyes of the Wild'

There are times when you meet a person and immediately feel at ease with them. It was like that the first time I met Dr. Jason Badridze—an instant sense of familiarity and warmth. I was in Georgia, the small republic in the Caucasus, writing about the country's efforts to protect its wilderness areas, when some of the nature reserve staff suggested that I meet him. They told me he had trained as a neurophysiologist and been professor of Ecology and Vertebrate Behavior at Tbilisi University. He was also the leading researcher on wolves in the Caucasus region, and he had raised orphaned wolf cubs himself and returned them to the wild.

Jason picked me up from the friend's flat where I always stayed in Tbilisi: in his fifties, compact and bearded, with dark oriental eyes and a beaky nose, his gaze was open and direct behind his glasses, and there was a vivid sense of humor dancing in their depths. He kept a pile of small change on the dashboard of his jeep, and whenever an elderly man or woman knocked on his window to beg at the traffic lights, he always passed them a few coins. "Hard times," he said briefly, "especially for the old."

Driving through the narrow streets of Tbilisi's old city,

past the houses of crumbling, saffron-colored stone with their enclosed, Moorish-style balconies on the upper levels, we soon discovered that we knew some of the same people.

"Ah, I am very happy that you know my blood brothers!" he exclaimed in his extravagant Georgian-Russian-accented English. Jason's "blood brothers" were several dedicated Russian biologists who raise orphaned bear cubs and wolf pups and return them to the wild. I had got to know them all when I visited their research center deep in the Russian taiga forest. The center had been founded by one of Jason's closest colleagues, the renowned brown bear biologist Professor Valentine Pazhetnov, whose son-in-law, Volodya, also raises orphaned wolf cubs.

That evening, as we sat in his flat talking over a bottle of the excellent Georgian red wine, Jason told me an episode from his life which I found so extraordinary, so unexpected and compelling that it could have come from the pages of a magical story rather than the life of a scientist.

When Jason was young, he had gone alone to a remote part of the Borjomi forest, in the mountains of the central Georgian Caucasus. He was looking for wolves. He wanted to find a wolf pack that would become so accustomed to his presence he could approach them closely and observe their daily lives.

At the time, this was new territory for a wolf biologist. It is very difficult to observe wild wolves in a forest—their lives are hidden among the trees and dense undergrowth, and revealed through their tracks and droppings and the remains of their kills rather than direct observation. Until radio collars and telemetry made it possible to track wolves from a distance, researchers learned about forest packs by following their trails on foot or ski and trying to understand the traces that they found.

It was rare for them to see a wild wolf at all. Long persecution has made wolves wary of human beings and they are very skilled at avoiding us. One American researcher, Doug Smith—who later took charge of reintroducing wolves to Yellowstone Park, in North America—spent ten field seasons traveling on foot and ski through wolf habitat on Isle Royale. During that entire period, he saw wolves from the ground only three times. Many researchers into animal behavior— also known as ethologists—watched wolves in captivity instead and studied their body language and ways of relating to each other. However, this approach to understanding wolves had an obvious disadvantage—wolves are wideranging animals and when they are confined, certain aspects of their behavior become distorted. To watch wolves behave naturally in the wild, a few researchers traveled to remote parts of the treeless Arctic tundra where it was possible to observe the wolves openly in summer.

Jason, though, wanted to do things differently, and he began by trying to understand things from the wolves' point of view.

"At first I had no idea how I could possibly make contact with those wolves or even come close enough to see them. I knew they were being hunted by the forest rangers because the only information I could find on them came from a government pamphlet telling hunters how they could track and kill them, so I decided that the first thing these wolves absolutely must understand is that I am not a danger to them.

I went to the rangers and I told them they were to keep out of that part of the forest. That wasn't easy! I used bad words; I talked very tough to them. Secondly, I decided that these wolves must always know my smell. So the whole time I was living in the forest I always wore the same clothes."

Jason followed the tracks and scat left by a small resident wolf pack and he began to put out deer meat for them at certain places in their territory. Then, in one sudden, heart-stopping moment, he came upon the adult male and female, the pack's mated pair. His first, instinctive reaction was to try to distract their attention away from him—he tossed the meat he was carrying before them on the ground.

The wolves ignored the meat, and the male took a few steps closer.

"When the male was a few yards away from me he stopped. I saw him look at me and it seemed to me that he was puzzled, that he could not understand what I wanted, why I did not seem to be a danger to him. Then the two wolves ran off into the trees and after they were gone I realized how frightened I'd been. I was shaking."

Some connection had been made during that brief meeting; in the months that followed it Jason regularly came upon the mated pair with the three others in their pack. The wolves, it seemed, were just as curious about this strangely benign, always solitary man whose presence had sent the hunters away. Finally Jason left the ranger's hut, which had been his base until then and began to live among them. He ran with them when they hunted and he slept near them on their rendezvous sites—the places where wolves gather while the pups are too young to travel very far with the adults.

"When these wolves had fully adapted to me, I lived with them. I took no tent. I had only the Caucasus shepherd's coat, which is made from felt. You can sleep outdoors even in rain and cold and stay dry and warm. I lived and worked alongside the wolves and when they accepted to let me follow them hunting, we often went for 30 or 40 kilometers a day together. I was young then, and I was very strong.

I lived for two years with these wolves in the Borjomi forest. During this time, I spent around 1,500 hours actively relating to them, sometimes at night, sometimes during the day. I never touched any of the wolves—I always stayed some distance away from them—and never once were they aggressive towards me. After some time, they let me take deer meat for myself from their kills—once they had eaten themselves, of course.

Those wolves were my teachers. Before I lived with them, I had been trying to analyze animal behavior even though I didn't know enough to understand what the behavior was really about."

I'd never seen a wild wolf when I first met Jason, and I had no direct experience of what he told me that evening, but I often thought about his story after I left Tbilisi. He had gone to the forest as a scientist: he wanted to observe as closely and accurately as he could how wolves really live in the wild. While he was among them, he'd been careful to respect the wolves' own space and keep certain important boundaries—

he'd never come too close and he'd never made any attempt to touch them. Yet his work had taken him beyond the limits of scientific observation of wild animals and plunged him into the stream of living relationship with them.

There was one image in particular that kept recurring in my mind—the figure of Jason asleep on the ground, alone in the darkness among the animals which, almost more than any other, have embodied certain human fears of the uncontrollable, instinctual, unpredictable wild. Few of us will ever see a wild wolf, but their presence still carries a powerful elemental charge into dreams and storytelling, and that image of Jason asleep on the ground among wolves, with its dreamlike, fairy-tale quality, spoke powerfully to me of trust and the possibility of making a new connection across the barriers of fear.

*   *   *

PART TWO

LISTENING AND CONNECTING

ON THE OTHER HAND

Heracles, I'm told
Heroically strangled a strong lion with his bare hands;
Androcles, on the other hand,
Gently drew a thorn from a wounded lion's paw.

Heracles, I'm told,
Heroically wore the dead lion's skin and head
as cloak and helmet;
Androcles, on the other hand,
Gently was saved from certain death
by his healed lion, alive.

© *Hilary Wilmshurst*

SHARING THE EARTH SPACE
Our relationships with other living creatures

Marian Van Eyk McCain
Adapted from the book 'Elderwoman: Reap the wisdom, feel the power, embrace the joy'

J. Allen Boone, in his beautiful, 1954 classic, *Kinship With All Life*, tells the story of his apprenticeship to a German Shepherd dog, and how, once he became humble enough to dispense with the mental categories of 'man' and 'dog,' let go of his preconceptions, and approach the project with a receptive mind, a whole new world opened for him. It is a wonderful story. But how many of us would have thought to apprentice ourselves to a dog?

We humans are such an arrogant species that we have even forgotten how closely related we are to all the other creatures who share our Earth, let alone how much all these other beings could teach us, if we listened.

My mother told me that my first non-human teacher was a dog called Patch, who helped my early efforts to walk upright by leading me patiently up and down the garden path with my hand in his mouth. I wish I could remember him. Unfortunately, I don't. However I do remember several other key teachers who have reached across the species gap to touch my life and change my way of seeing.

One of the most memorable was a teacher I met one

summer, quite unexpectedly, in the mountains of south-eastern Australia. I shall always remember our first encounter.

It was a hot, still day; a day of heat haze and blue sky, of eucalyptus scent and the shrilling of cicadas. Inside the cabin, I was eating a solitary lunch, and reading a book, glad to be in the shade.

In that valley, summer breezes often begin around midday, bringing cooler afternoons. So when I heard something rustle outside, I looked hopefully out at the peach tree, expecting to see its leaves fluttering. To my surprise they were motionless. Even as I stared, the rustling happened again. Intrigued, I put down my half-eaten sandwich and crossed to the door.

Outside, all was still. No breeze. Just the shimmer of heat on the brick paving. There was another rustle, right by my feet. Then I saw him. A full-sized snake, slithering away towards the bookcase.

I screamed, and leaped outside.

Then, dismayed, I realized my predicament. Inside my cabin, was an Australian brown snake, one of the world's most seriously venomous reptiles. And here was I, on the porch.

I peered in gingerly. "Excuse me," I said. "This is backwards. It is you who are supposed to be out here, not me. Would you mind changing places? Please?"

He took his time; made a full circuit of the cabin, examining everything, his tongue flicking. Under the table where a few moments ago I had innocently sat reading my book, under the wood stove, under the dresser. "Oh please," I pleaded, "don't go in the bedroom." I had no idea what I would do if he decided to hide under the bed and stay there.

But he didn't. After a full inspection of the room, he poured himself elegantly out of the door, turned, and disappeared under the cabin.

I sat down, trembling.

Was this how it must have been, I wondered, for Cave Woman? And what of Cave Man, hunting in his bare feet on the forest path, knowing he was potentially both predator and prey and every rustle could be a hungry tiger?

Our tigers are paper tigers nowadays. The only predators the profiteers, hungry for our dollar. We have only ourselves and each other to fear, and our own fearsome creations. Our modern fears rarely shock us awake into the sudden awareness of mortal danger and thereby into the fullness of the present moment. Rather than powering us for that leap to safety or solution, they send us scrabbling for the remote among the sofa cushions and slipping into a virtual world, suspending our minds, till they are neither weary nor wakeful; merely dulled.

Even in that TV-less cabin, with all the mountain scenery to savour, it was still easy to drift away into those endless rehearsals for the future and re-hashings of the past that preoccupy the ever restless mind. So although I knew he was there, living under my floorboards, half a leg length away, I still forgot the snake. And every time he reappeared, the sight of him shocked me awake again.

One day he was curled up near the outdoor shower. Another time he crossed beneath me as I stood on the stepladder. He had a favourite dozing spot under the apricot tree, and I usually looked for him there. Nevertheless, one morning I forgot, and almost stepped on him. He reared up, and once again my feet left the ground in a hurry. As before, our sudden meeting left me trembling. But as I felt into the trembling, I knew that it was not only fear. There was also an exhilaration. A strange feeling of rightness. As though I were sharing some deep and primeval experience with those ancient, cave-dwelling ancestors.

I began to feel gratitude—almost affection—for this deadly teacher in the grass, with his silent, repeated message. Wake up. Stay awake. Stay in the moment. Stay in your body. Feel your aliveness. Every step you take, take it with awareness. Any moment, you may die. Life is precious, amazing, an adventure.

I nicknamed him Mr. Slitheroe. Whenever I walked outside, I would stamp my foot and call out to him, warning him of my presence, so we could both maintain our necessary distance. I made up a song about him, and I sang it to him as I pottered in the garden.

My partner had been away for several weeks. On his return I told him of the new neighbour below us.

"What do you think we should do about it?" he asked.

"Nothing," I heard myself answer. "Mr. Slitheroe is my Zen master. Every time I forget to live in the moment, he calls me back to awareness with a jolt. I know it sounds weird, but I actually like having him here. I would miss him now. Can you understand that?"

He understood.

Our human neighbours were less understanding.

"You'd be better off hitting him over the head," said one.

"The only good snake," said another, in that laconic way

Australians talk, "…is a dead snake."

"You're being irresponsible," said a third.

But leave him we did.

As the days grew shorter and the sun lost its fierceness, he left, migrating to who knows where for the cooler, wetter times. We left too.

I knew that the following summer, someone else would be living in the cabin, picking apricots from the tree, eating their lunch at the table. I wondered if one day they would hear a mysterious rustle or see a sudden movement in the grass. And if that happened, I wondered what those people would do. They may not share my bizarre notion that it can be strangely useful to live a whole summer with a snake-shaped Zen master under the floorboards. However, I knew that I could not alter their destiny, nor Mr. Slitheroe's. We always have to trust that others will make whatever choice is best for them. Including snakes. Whether consciously or otherwise, we each follow the path that is right for us, with all its twists and turns.

If I had killed that slim brown creature who chose to live with us that summer, I would have had another set of feelings to deal with. A different lesson, but perhaps equally valuable. D. H. Lawrence wrote about that experience in his wonderful poem, 'Snake': the hasty, automatic reaction, the guilt that followed his recognition of the impulse to destroy the snake who came to drink at his water trough.

The Killing Question

The whole issue of our predatory nature and the killing of other creatures is a thorny one. I am a vegetarian, but I have no quarrel with those who would kill an animal to eat it. We are omnivorous mammals, after all, and meat has long been part of our diet. One of my two reasons for being a vegetarian is a personal one, which is that the killing of other creatures is so painful for me that I cannot do it. Since I cannot do it, it feels morally wrong to turn my back and expect others to do it for me. My simple guideline is that whatever I would have no qualms about removing from its environment myself, I permit myself to eat. Since I can easily pull a carrot or cut a cabbage, or even pluck an oyster off a rock, these I can eat. I could not bring myself to blast a bird out of the sky, to hook a struggling fish out of the water or to plunge a lobster into a boiling vat, so these I refuse to eat. People less squeamish than me can go hunting, and happily devour the flesh of their kill. I have no problem with this. Neither do I have problems with people who can stand, unflinching, in an abattoir, and go home to a blood-red steak. My judgement is reserved for those who recoil in horror at the thought of such a scene and yet can buy pieces of a dead animal wrapped in plastic from the supermarket and draw some sort of mental curtain over the thought of that animal's slaughter. To me, each time we do something like that, we lose awareness. We lose aliveness. We step into the dull, hypnotized world of moral unconsciousness.

My second reason for being a vegetarian is an ideological one, based on the current size of the human population. I believe more people would be able to eat if we all ate low on the food chain. Millions of acres now devoted to cattle grazing or to fodder crops so that the lucky few can eat meat, could be used to grow food for the many who now go to bed hungry.

Since I realize that human beings are biologically adapted to eating a varied diet which includes meat as well as all the other things, I have never claimed that meat-eating is less 'natural' than vegetarianism. Nevertheless, I do maintain that meat-eating removed from the context of hunting, where hunter and hunted are in relationship, to the context of the modern supermarket, where one is free to claim an animal's body while having no relationship with—or even conscious awareness of—the animal who once lived in it, is unnatural, alienating and destructive of the soul.

Making Comparisons

When we talk about our relationship with other species, we risk falling into another trap which is more subtle—and much more pleasant to discuss—but equally alienating. This is the trap of anthropomorphism. Of attributing human thoughts, feelings and attitudes to other creatures. All those who have lived closely with an animal, be it dog, cat, horse or some other creature, will have been aware of that animal's individual personality, its likes and dislikes, its foibles and phobias and wide range of moods and emotions.

But just because these are recognizable, it does not mean that we fully understand them. In our partial understanding, we have developed the habit of patronizing other species rather than fully respecting and honouring their otherness.

Through our scientific knowledge of that amazing organ, the cerebral cortex, which has given human beings the capacity for abstract thought, a rarely questioned assumption has arisen. This is the assumption that evolution operates rather like an automobile factory, with each year's model being superior in all ways to the previous model. So a starfish is superior to, or 'better than' a one-celled organism, a lizard is 'better than' a starfish, a rabbit is 'better than' a lizard, a monkey is 'better than' a rabbit and a human being is 'better than' a monkey—or anything else.

Even with respect to cars this reasoning is not really valid. While today's fast, sleek machine is speedier and more manoeuvrable than Henry Ford's early models, it is also trickier to repair, uses up more resources in its manufacture, running and repair, dents more easily and causes more accidents. So superiority always depends on what particular factors we are measuring. When it comes to comparing people with each other, we know that it is invalid to make general comparisons. Certainly I can say, from looking at our golf handicaps, that I am a better golfer than you. You, who have won six prizes for cake decorating, can rightly claim to be better at frosting cakes than I am. You are taller, I am fairer, you can hold a tune better than I can, I can run faster...and so on. But neither of us is a superior being. As human beings, we consider ourselves equal.

So I believe that the same thing applies to other creatures. In a game of Scrabble, I would beat a seal every time. But in a swimming contest, the seal would leave me far behind. I am more computer literate than a dolphin or a bat, but my sonar navigation skills are virtually zero. Human beings are less co-operative than bees, less faithful than swans, and most of us are far less stoical than the male emperor penguin who spends the entire Antarctic winter standing in one spot with an egg resting on his feet, with his mate away at sea and blizzards swirling around him.

We are not, as is generally assumed, the end point of evolution. Evolution is more in the shape of a mighty tree, with main branches and minor branches and twigs. We are simply one of the furthest twigs from the trunk, that's all.

This does not mean that we have no right to kill other creatures for our own survival. Forms of life have been swallowing other forms of life since Day One - or, more correctly, since a certain day, around fifteen billion years after the Big Bang. That was the day—roughly one billion years ago—when, after three billion years or so of cells minding their own business and living on each other's waste products, a mutation led to the first swallowing of one, live, one-celled organism by another. And life has fed on life ever since. Which puts us here, now, at the top of the food chain.

However, being on top of the food chain means only that we are on top of the food chain. It does not give us the moral right to claim any kind of overall superiority. Nor, since we are conscious animals and aware of our actions, does it give us the right to exploit other forms of life heedlessly. The problem, I believe, is in the fact that we humans destroy other creatures not simply for our basic food needs, but for sport, for fun, for convenience, and as a side effect of our profligate way of life.

Apart from the chosen creatures who share our homes as 'pets,' the ones we enslave as commodities, to eat, experiment upon or use as spare body parts, the opportunistic creatures who colonize our houses, bodies and gardens against our will and with whom we do constant battle, such as rats, fleas, lice, flies, dust mites and garden 'pests,' our culture seems to view the function of all the others—the ones who live in the wild or in zoos—as the entertainment of humans. Now that we have succeeded in removing ourselves from the dangers of predators, Nature has become pretty wallpaper instead of being the matrix of our lives. Something to drive around in on Sundays or watch documentaries about from our armchairs.

For me, part of living lightly and sustainably on the Earth has been the deliberate attempt to re-insert myself into that matrix. One way of doing that is to examine these fundamental issues about how we relate to non-human creatures and to change our thinking about them. In trying to let go of my old, stereotyped ways of seeing other creatures and relating to them, I find myself learning unexpected lessons, as I did in my relationship with Mr. Slitheroe. Not only that, but life becomes suddenly richer, deeper, more meaningful.

We have co-evolved with other life-forms. Our bodies are made from the same substances. Our minds have been shaped by interaction with them since the very beginnings of humanity. We are inextricably related. It is not 'us' and 'them' it is a huge, universal 'we.'

In the Native American, Australian aboriginal and some other cultures, this connection is not only honoured but taken a step further by the whole concept of totems. The totemic relationship between a group of humans and a particular species of animal is one of a special belonging—a mystical and spiritual bonding. Our sacred kinship with the rest of Earth's creatures goes back a very long way indeed.

The change which is needed is for human beings to let go of exploitative and anthropomorphic attitudes to other creatures and substitute feelings of love, admiration and, above all—respect.

Respecting the Other

"What is needed is a complete revolution in the way we deal with other species. Do not expect, then, to find me in any way 'balanced' on the question: this is not really an issue on which there are two sides."

—Colin McGinn.

Back in 1966, in his now-famous paper presented to the American Association for the Advancement of Science, historian Lyn White JR. suggested that our religion has a lot to answer for in terms of our destruction of the environment. White said that he believed our arrogant exploitation of the natural world would continue until we rejected the misinterpretation of the bible that made us believe Nature has no existence except to serve us.

Since the roots of our trouble are so largely religious, the remedy must also be essentially religious, whether we call it that or not. We must re-think and refeel our destiny.

White was speaking about precisely the change in thinking that I have been discussing here. We need to move away from anthropocentric (human-centered) thinking, in the same way that we had to move away from our former belief that the sun revolved around the Earth. Nothing will change until we do. I believe that the principle we need to call upon in relation to other creatures, as well as other human beings, is the principle of respect.

Every day at Monkey Mia, on the west coast of Australia, wild dolphins swim to the shore to greet humans. If you stand there quietly, in the shallows, and wait patiently, they will come. I shall never forget the first time I watched a dolphin approach. She swam slowly in front of the row of people, like a general inspecting a parade. Turned on her side, one eye out of the water, she stared up at them, fixing them with her gaze. Excited, I watched her swim towards me, along the row, imagining how our eyes would meet and some magical, New Age-type communion of souls would take place.

Wrong. It was not at all like I had imagined. I can see it now, that dark, intense, penetrating eye meeting mine. But instead of a feeling of connection, I was suddenly overwhelmed by the recognition of our utter and complete difference. And what grew and swelled in me in that moment was a feeling I have never lost. It was the feeling of profound respect. She was forever a dolphin, from the sea world. I was forever a woman, from the land world. Our worlds could never merge, they could only meet at this amazing, respectful edge. I don't know if the same was true for her, but for me, the existence of that edge—that very otherness of hers—has made my whole world ten times more beautiful. It was one of the most precious gifts I have ever been given.

*   *   *

RETURN TO THE LISTENING PLACE

Clea Danaan

Adapted and partially excerpted from her book
'Voices of the Earth: The Path of Green Spirituality'

I moved frequently as a child, my family always in search
of cheaper rent or a shorter commute to work. One of our
houses floated in a moat of blackberry brambles, overlooking
Skagit Bay to the west. Second growth forest and a tangle
of blackberries filled the sizeable stretch between us and our
nearest neighbor. Across the street beckoned an empty lot,
cleared of most of its timber but just passable to adventurous
eight-year-olds. Here I discovered some of my first spirit
teachers: a circle of granite boulders. Following some ancient
call, I named them Grandmother, Grandfather, Aunt and
Uncle. I did not yet know the word 'sacred,' but I felt a sweet
and solemn power in this circle of boulders. I played amidst
their powerful energy, sheltered by the draping branches of
Douglas fir. To me the pine needles padding the ground were
magic. I would lean against the rough granite and whisper the
stones my secrets, flaking off bits of lichen with my fingernails.
I felt them listening. The hum of their rock consciousness
surrounded me.

From these rocks, the blackberry brambles around my

house, and the bay to the west I learned that stones have personalities, that the tides and sea weather dialogue with the land, and that blackberry brambles bind and protect. As I grew, these wild beings became a part of my days, my breath, my heart. The seasons of rain and sun, the prick of blackberry thorn, the call of frogs in a nearby stream, all rooted me deeply in the language of the land. Though we moved on, I carried these natural songs within. They taught me how to listen.

Many years later, a boyfriend and I explored the Washington Park Arboretum in Seattle, playing with the energy of trees. We rested our hands on tree trunks and felt a spiral of energy pulsing sun-wise toward the sky. We wandered through the Arboretum, drawn to one tree or another, comparing notes, until we happened upon a ring of forty-foot tall sequoias. As I stood in the center of the circle of trees, my entire body hummed, vibrating as if I had drunk too much strong coffee. I inhaled deeply, tuning into the moist soil beneath my feet, the stretch above of waxy green fronds, and the vast strength and vitality of these powerful trees. These sequoias share land with rhododendrons, ferns, and moss-infused grassy hills. In their midst one can hear traffic, but also sink into the ancient quiet of the waiting stones and spreading green. The land around them, though cultivated, has its own wildness that has taken over the Arboretum after many years of Pacific Northwest rains.

Without words, the trees spoke to me: Let the flow of life carry you. The land supports you, cradles you, as it does us. We are one Earth, made up of distinct organisms, each fulfilling our unique tasks as humans, as trees. Come spend time with us, learn to listen, and the flow of your life will unfold toward the highest good of all.

Several years later, a flock of birds offered a similar message. After an intense weekend studying Expressive Arts Therapy at a retreat center, I sought fresh air and solitude. The nearby wetland beckoned. I crossed the driveway and surrounding meadow and into a copse of alders. The spot reminded me of my childhood stone circle, surrounded by blackberries with a backdrop of fir. Winter cattails poked through the mud, brown alder leaves pasted the soggy ground, and though it was after noon, hoar frost still lurked at the clearing edges. Blackberry bushes in winter have their own unique smell, sweet and grassy and brown, often laced with the clay scent of popping wetland soil. I let the smell soak in. My awareness expanded into the land around me. My body seemed to expand as well, as I became a part of the wetland. I followed the edge of the creek as it meandered through faded marsh grass and winter-bare alders until I came across a thin stump, marked with the telltale grooves of beaver teeth. Alder shavings littered the ground. I wondered how recently this engineering beaver had been here, working on his or her house of saplings. The teeth marks looked fresh.

As I stood at the edge of the slow-moving stream, a lace of branches all around, a covey of little brown birds landed in the tree in front of me. They hopped curiously from branch to branch, seeming to look right at me. I felt like Snow White, friend of forest creatures. I actually held out my hand in invitation, imagining one little finch might fulfill the fantasy and alight upon my finger. They seemed so tame and friendly. None of the birds took me up on my offer, but fluttered around me for some time with a chorus of curious chirps. At some signal cryptic to me they scampered off into the wetland. They had been so pointedly interested in me, I guessed that someone must have regularly fed them birdseed at this spot.

I later asked one of the women who lived at the retreat center if someone fed birds out by the beaver-chewed stump. She knew the spot I meant, rolling her eyes at the nuisance of beavers, but said no one fed birds that far from the house. I had been visited by the little flock for no other reason than to say hello. I believe this was because my work at the retreat had left me peacefully empty, able to still my mind and enter into the vibration of the wetland. I had become a part of the wetland. I had returned to the listening space of my childhood and opened to the flow of the land.

The trees and stones, rivers and birds call to me: Listen. An ancient relationship with plants and stones pulses in my blood like the wildness that reclaims cultivated lands, a relationship that I seek to cultivate even in a city or amidst suburban sprawl. When I slow down and tune into my subtle senses, I find a whole new level of being where plants talk and stones offer companionship. The world around me, whether a city lot or a stretch of protected wilderness, suddenly becomes alive in a whole new way. I find teachers and companions that help me learn what it means to live on the planet Earth. I draw on this sacred relationship each day as I mother, garden, write, play. I become like a tree, growing my roots ever deeper as above I seek the light. While I find this awareness of the sacredness of Nature at times makes life more difficult (as it often conflicts so deeply with modern life), I feel more whole, more real, by letting this flow of life be my guide, carrying me along my journey.

I can't help but wonder what the world would be like if we all developed this deeper listening—to Nature, each other, and ourselves. What would it mean if children were raised to honour stones as ancestors? If we all consciously knew the energetic signatures of the trees that surround our homes? If song birds were regarded as individuals? And how can I invite others into this deeper listening without seeming preachy? Once a person knows the wisdom of the land, really feels it deep in his or her bones, the wisdom becomes a truth. Until then my words may seem silly, or worse, conceited moralization. All I can do, I suppose, is to invite experience through stories. To offer others the skills of listening and then let the natural world speak her song.

*　　*　　*

TELEPATHY

Rupert Sheldrake

In his book *The Lost World of the Kalahari*, Sir Laurens van der Post described how bushmen were in telepathic contact over enormous distances. They themselves compared their method of communication to the white man's telegraph or 'wire.' On one occasion van der Post had been out hunting with a group of bushmen. As they were heading back in Land-Rovers laden with eland meat, he asked how the people back at the camp would react when they learned of their success. One of his companions replied, "They already know. They know by wire…We bushmen have a wire here" … he tapped his chest … "that brings us news." Sure enough, when they approached the camp, the people were singing the eland song and preparing to give the hunters the greatest of welcomes.

By contrast, educated people in the West are usually brought up to believe that telepathy does not exist. Like other so-called psychic phenomena, it is dismissed as an illusion. Nevertheless, even in modern Britain, most people have had personal experiences that seem telepathic, most frequently in connection with telephones. For example, Janet Ward, of Budleigh Salterton, told me, "For a long time, I have had a feeling of telepathy with my two daughters whom I am very close to. I start thinking about them just before the phone rings. It happens too with friends. I'm always saying 'I was just thinking about you' when I answer the phone to them."

Perceptive Pets

Telepathy seems even more common with dogs and cats than with people. For example, many cat owners have found that their animals seem to sense when they are planning to take them to the vet, even before they have got out the carrying basket or given any apparent clues as to their intention. They disappear.

In the course of several years' research with pets, I heard so many of these stories that I made a survey of all the vets in north London to find out what they had noticed. All but one said people often cancelled appointments because they could not find their cat. The remaining clinic had given up an appointment system for cats because there were so many cancellations; people just had to turn up with their animal.

Some people say their dogs know when they are going to be taken for a walk, even at unusual times, and even when they are in a different room, out of sight and hearing. The dogs detect their owners' intentions, and bound into the room in eager anticipation.

One of the commonest and most testable claims about dogs and cats is that they know when their owners are coming home. In some cases they seem to anticipate their owners' arrivals by ten minutes or more, even at non-routine times, and even when people travel in unfamiliar vehicles.

The dog I have investigated in most detail is a terrier called Jaytee, who belongs to Pam Smart, in Ramsbottom, Greater Manchester. Pam's family noticed that he seemed to anticipate her returns by going to wait at the window up to 45 minutes before she came home. He started waiting around the time she set off.

In more than 100 trials, we videotaped the area by the window where Jaytee waited during Pam's absences, providing a continuous, timecoded record of his behaviour. She went at least five miles away. To find out if Jaytee was simply reacting to the sound of her car, she returned by train or by taxi. He still knew when she was coming.

Jaytee's reactions were not a matter of routine, but occurred whenever Pam came home at randomly selected times signalled through a telephone pager. Jaytee behaved in the same way when he was tested repeatedly by sceptics anxious to debunk his abilities.

The evidence shows that Jaytee was reacting to Pam's intention to come home even when she was miles away. We have since replicated this work with other dogs. Telepathy seems the only hypothesis that can account for the facts. (For more details, see the latest edition of my book *Dogs That Know When Their Owners Are Coming Home: And Other Unexplained Powers of Animals*.)

If domestic animals are telepathic with their human owners, then it seems likely that animals are telepathic with each other in the wild, for example within packs of wolves. Telepathy may have evolved as a means of communication that enables members of animal groups to keep in touch at a distance.

In modern human societies we now have telephones, but telepathy has not gone away. Someone's intention to make a call often seems to be picked up telepathically before the call itself.

Telephone Telepathy

But is apparent telephone telepathy really telepathic? Could there be a more mundane explanation? People may think of others from time to time for no particular reason, and if someone they are thinking of then calls, this may be a matter of chance. People may simply forget all the times they think of someone who does not ring.

This is a reasonable possibility, but there is no evidence for it. The only way to resolve the question scientifically is by experiment.

I have developed a simple procedure in which subjects receive a call from one of four different callers at a prearranged time. The subjects nominate the callers themselves, usually close friends or family members. They do not know who will be calling in any given test, because the caller is picked at random by the experimenter by the throw of a die. Subjects have to guess who the caller is before picking up the receiver. By chance they would be right about one time in four, or 25 per cent of the time. In many of these trials, the participants are videotaped continuously to make sure that they do not receive any other telephone calls or emails that could give them any clues.

My colleagues and I have so far conducted more than 800 trials. The average success rate is 42 per cent, very significantly above the chance level of 25 per cent, with statistical odds against chance of trillions to one.

We have also carried out a series of trials in which two of the four callers were familiar, and the other two were strangers, whose names the participants knew, but whom they had not met. With familiar callers, the success rate was more than 50 per cent, highly significant statistically. With strangers it was near the chance level, in agreement with the observation that telepathy typically takes place between people who share emotional or social bonds.

In addition, we have found that these effects do not fall off with distance. In some of our tests the callers were in Australia or New Zealand, but the subjects identified them just as well as callers nearby.

Unfortunately, in most of their laboratory research on telepathy, parapsychologists have used senders and receivers who are complete strangers, creating poor conditions for success. With participants who are bonded to each other the results are generally far more impressive.

Telepathy continues to evolve. One of its latest manifestations is the telepathic email. People think of someone who shortly afterwards sends them an email. We have done more than 700 tests on email telepathy, following a similar design to the telephone tests, with a success rate of 43 per cent, highly significant statistically. These tests can now be done online through my website, and readers are welcome to try for themselves.

We do not yet understand telepathy; but it is unscientific to dismiss it or pretend it doesn't exist. Only by exploring it can we find out more. We still have much to learn about the nature of minds, and telepathy offers vital clues. It implies that we are more interconnected than we usually assume.

*   *   *

PART THREE

LEARNING
AND HEALING

LESSONS FROM FROGS

Marian Van Eyk McCain
Adapted from the book
'The Lilypad List: 7 steps to the simple life'

I shine my torch on the garden pond.
A carpet of duckweed covers almost the entire surface of the water, still and smooth and green as a golf course, broken here and there by the serrated leaf of a water parsnip. Around the edges, the honey-coloured rocks are almost hidden now, in a tangle of wild plants.

I am searching for snails and slugs. For although they are welcome to feast at will here, in this wild corner of my tiny, hillside garden, I cannot risk that some time later on this long, dark night, they will make the two metre journey from the edge of here to the place where the wildness ends and the cabbage patch begins.

There seem to be neither snails nor slugs abroad here tonight. But the swooping arc of my torch beam catches something else. A tiny pair of eyes, just above the water level. And another, and another... Small faces, still and solemn, under rakish little hats of duckweed.

My pond is full of frogs again.

Every year, they come.

I never think to peel back the mat of water parsnip roots and duckweed to look for spawn or tadpoles in the early spring. So every year the fully-formed frogs seem to appear from nowhere, as though they had parachuted in from somewhere else. Yet I know they were born here, deep within the brown-green water of this little pond. Here they hatched and swam, used up their tails and grew their legs. Here, right here, beneath the duckweed and beneath my awareness, their miracle of transformation happened and their frog lives began, unquestioned and unseen. This is their taken-for-granted world and this, to them, is all the world there is. Beyond the rocks, beyond the nettles, lies the far edge of the Universe.

I swing my torch again and count them. Six pairs of eyes—or is it seven? Ah, there is another, almost hidden in the water parsnips. It feels like one of those 'can you find it?' puzzles we loved as children. You stare and stare at the page and suddenly there is a tiger in the undergrowth. Or a frog in the water parsnips. And you wonder how you could have missed it earlier.

They blend in well, their browny-green colours blending with the natural colours of the vegetation. In fact, had it been daylight, and the colours more vivid, I doubt I would have seen them at all. For these frogs are made to fit their surroundings. Only Nature's clever use of camouflage has kept them and their ancestors from the greedy beaks of herons.

Are there herons who would eat us alive, too, if we failed to fit in as well with our surroundings as these frogs fit with theirs?

I think there are. And I think the herons are already here, already hungry. For as far as I am aware, there has never, in the history of our world, been a creature which could survive for very long if it failed to fit in properly with its surroundings. We are the first, foolish creatures to try and bend the rules of Nature. And our arrogance may be our undoing.

So the herons of global warming and climate change, the herons of water shortage and of desertification, they and all the other herons will fly in from the outer edges of the Universe and catch and eat us, and the big experiment will be over.

But what if we changed our ways now? Will it be too late? I don't know. No-one knows. But we can surely try. We can learn to live properly in our own small pond, blending in with the rest of Nature, living simply and being happy.

I am not sure if these frogs are happy. Their eyes are unblinking and their tiny faces are inscrutable. But they are still and quiet and living patiently, peacefully and—as far as I can tell—totally in the here and now. I have noticed that on the odd occasions when I can manage do that, it seems to bring me a certain kind of happiness which I should like to feel more often—all the time, if possible.

How do they manage to stay so still, these frogs?

As I hold them in my torch beam, they remain motionless, unblinking. From where I stand, on the far side of the pond from them, I am too far away to discern the telltale movements of their little throats as they breathe. So for all I know, they could be small pieces of wood, carved in the shape of frogs' heads, with tiny knots in the place of eyes. Or they could be merely a trick of my own eyes—an optical illusion.

I know, though, that when they do move, it is so lightning fast that my slow eyes cannot even catch it. You have to be quick if your favourite dinner is a fast-flying insect and you have a bare millisecond in which to grab it as it whizzes by.

Evolution has given these frogs specialised cells in the retinas of their eyes, which are designed to pick out movement. A frog, I have heard, can starve to death sitting on top of a pile of dead flies. You would want to shake that frog, wouldn't you? You would want to say "Look there—flies! Eat them! Don't be so *stupid!*"

And here am I, with my clever, convoluted brain, every bit as much a child of evolution as these frogs. Yet I, too, could starve to death in the midst of plenty if I did not recognise what I am sitting on as an alternative source of nourishment. Evolution encouraged me to make tools, to speak, to explore and to create. It has programmed me to search and to seek, to learn and to grow. But if I and all my people, in our search for knowledge and our love of acquiring new things, and our clever use of tools have come to the point where that very tendency is beginning to endanger our lives, we are in big trouble. What if we are so busy watching for the next bit of amazing technology to come whizzing by and rescue us from our predicament that we fail to recognise that we are sitting on a pile of simple treasure? What if we are so hooked on getting all our energy from oil that we sit and wring our hands as the oil wells run dry rather than turning to the limitless energy of the sun and wind and tides?

What if we are so accustomed to finding everything we need at the supermarket that we forget how to grow food? If we don't rediscover the skills of our ancestors—the traditional, non-polluting ways of meeting our needs for food, clothing, shelter and entertainment—restore their value, update them for our times and learn to live more simply and sustainably, we shall perish—and take the poor frogs with us.

These frogs in my pond are so still, so quiet. I envy them their stillness, their quietness, their patience. I want more of that for myself. Since I have come to live here, I notice that I am appreciating silence and stillness more and more. The dark peacefulness of the nights is so soothing and refreshing. And in that night stillness, I can hear wonderful sounds: the wheezy bark of a fox, several fields away: the low calling of an owl: a cricket's chirp. And the sound of the breeze stirring the leaves of the hawthorn tree outside my window.

There is a small toad at the base of that tree tonight, and I just miss stepping on him—or her—as I make my way back to the house after slug patrol. The toad is probably on slug patrol too. I like toads as much as I like their cousins, the frogs. When I dug the pond, I made it as deep as I could and at the bottom I placed some old flower pots on their sides, weighted with stones. I know that toads like such places to hibernate. Maybe this little toad will spend the winter in my pond. I would like that. I pick the little creature up and carry him or her, cool and heavy in my hand, to the safety of a nearby flower bed, speaking my gratitude for all the slugs s/he has already caught and my hope for much future success in the slug hunt. The toad, dark as night, sidles away under the nasturtiums. The sweet peas nearby fill my nostrils with delight, and I pause in the doorway to take another sniff. For smells, too, are enhanced by the stillness of night.

Once, when I lived in the tropics, there was a small gardenia bush which grew right outside my bedroom window. Its scent was so heavy and so luscious that it almost kept me awake. In its branches lived a bright green tree frog which chirped all night in the same spot, catching night-flying moths and other winged things which flitted around the house, attracted by the dim light on the porch. Looking back, I think frogs have always been around, calling to me to notice them. I am glad I am noticing now—and listening to their small, quiet messages. I have so much to learn from them.

*   *   *

ALL OUR COMPANIONS

Three stories from veterinary acupuncturist
Suzannah Stacey

1. Lost in Translation

Lately, I have noticed a theme developing in my working life as a veterinary acupuncturist, namely one of communication, a concept much discussed amongst human lifestyle gurus. I have been guilty of not giving the subject sufficient thought with regard to my animal patients, taking much for granted in my understanding of animal communications.

My recent awakening began at the dog training club; on the first evening, the class was instructed that the word 'no' was not appropriate in a training setting. The trainer explained: if your dog is doing something that you would prefer it not to do, give him or her something better to do rather than endlessly shouting 'no' at the hapless creature.

Needless to say I then spent the next half an hour uttering 'no' half a dozen times as a kind of nervous reflex, followed by a hasty apology to the trainer as I tried to get the hang of this seemingly complex new approach to dog communication.

The theme of communicating continued when I signed up for a short course aimed at helping vets create a stress-free practice environment for their canine patients. Most of the four hours focused on reading dog body language, and it quickly became apparent that, despite being in a room full of people who worked with animals day and night, communication at this level was not our forte, and we all made a bit of a dog's breakfast of interpreting the slides of various dog's facial expressions and body positioning.

An episode the following day emphasised for me the shortfall in relating to my own patients' communications. I was visiting a horse that I have been treating for several years for a previous injury and subsequent arthritis in a hind leg. It was obvious as soon as I arrived that the horse was not in the best of moods, and he fidgeted and scraped the ground with his foot repeatedly.

"Shall I move him to where he can see his field buddy?" his human asked, slightly embarrassed by her horse's display of unsettled behaviour.

"Don't worry" I replied, confident to trust in the horse's training and experience of people that he would do me no harm. Indeed, he didn't, and as always let me insert my needles without so much as a flicker, still shuffling his feet in between times. Just as I relaxed after placing a dozen needles into him, he turned his head and quick as a flash pulled out the nearest needle from his shoulder! Instantly, his human and I reacted, checking his mouth and the ground nearby for the giveaway red needle handle.

After a few minutes of focused searching, it was discovered some distance away from the treatment area. I breathed a sigh of relief, and as I journeyed home that evening, I recalled how persistently this horse had tried to communicate with me and how little attention I had paid to his signals. With so many simple things to try to put him more at ease, such as moving him nearer to the company of another horse, my listening skills had definitely been taking a holiday that day. So instead, he became the only horse I have ever known during my career to have removed a needle during a treatment. Point taken! The time has come for me to start really hearing the voice of my animal friends.

2. Rescuing Ollie

On a beautiful sunny summer's day two years ago, I cradled Stan's beautiful silky black head in my hands for one last time and kissed my faithful Labrador goodbye. This, my final selfless deed as human companion and guardian carried with it a weight of guilt as heavy as the sky, even though it was so clearly the right decision to make I was blessed to have many sympathetic and compassionate people share my sense of loss over the next few months, and time allowed me to adjust to holding Stan in my heart as a beautiful memory.

On quiet days I would pause in my garden and consider whether to look for another dog in need of a 'forever home.' I pushed the idea away each time, distracted by worries about the commitment of time needed and how this would impact on every area of my life. The wisdom of my own psyche, however, started to focus on this idea a little more, and I found myself surfing the internet late at night looking at rescue dogs in need of a loving home. One or two became more active enquiries, but for one reason or another fell by the wayside. I was philosophical about the news each time as I was not yet certain if I was ready to make this commitment again. As the New Year came and went, another email enquiry went off, and this time a phone call came back, asking if I wanted to meet Ollie, a 'large whippet' currently in foster care locally. I agreed, calming my logical mind with the thought that meeting him wouldn't necessarily mean I had agreed to anything more. Intuition took the lead, however, and I knew that he was to come home with me as soon as he jumped out of the white van, gently and cautiously waving his tail.

Ollie's homecoming gave me a strong, constant sense of having a stranger in the house. For some reason I found him unfathomable, and his initial responses to me and to his surroundings were difficult to predict or interpret. Every day I mused on the changes that we both were making to accommodate sharing a life together.

Enrolling in an outdoor training club, I had the joy of watching this elegant dog experience freedom for the first time in many months, and he galloped about the woodland paths with such joy in the simple act of running, that I felt his sheer love of movement as if I were running with him too.

The trainer, who is a caring and knowledgeable soul, answered my question about how to relate to this free spirit with a simple question of her own. 'Why', she asked me, 'does your dog need you'? As Ollie can catch his own food with ease, and find water with little effort, I was at a loss to suggest what I was going to provide for him that would keep him bound to me. "Safety," she declared with a grin. "It's your job to keep him safe." This simple statement changed everything, and every night as I settle down to sleep I silently speak to him my intention to do my very best to keep him safe. That is my promise to him.

Ollie brought with him a handful of medical issues and in the process of seeking healing for this damaged soul I researched using the Bach flower remedies, acupuncture, conventional medicine, homoeopathy, and hydrotherapy to address his problems. Each therapist I meet gives me a sense of hope and joy that Ollie is moving closer to becoming physically and emotionally whole and free. Every practitioner has some new knowledge or insight for me to absorb; united with them in the goal of healing Ollie, I feel supported and bonded to my fellow humans. Days when I visit someone who is helping me to heal him, or when we make progress in our training or discover some new walk together are always my happiest days. With them return some of my best memories of happy times with Stan, Cassie, Ringo, Sandy and all the other animals I have been fortunate enough to share part of my life with.

As I reflect back upon my journey with this remote young dog to whom life has already dealt some cruel blows, I become certain that the reason why he came into my life is simply because having him here makes me, in so many ways, a better human being.

3. A Smack for Sam

Life in practice is not always plain sailing, as I discovered a few weeks ago when spending time with one of my smaller patients, a little Chihuahua cross named Sam.

The problem arose when I was about to load the car and depart after giving him a successful treatment for a leg injury. Sam was excited about having some personal attention and started to express his joyful feelings by jumping about near the car. This earned him some stern words from his human and a smack on his bottom too.

When I got home I thought about that smack and Sam's tiny size and it troubled me. Over 20 years ago when I was training my own young Jack Russell, the trainer spoke to our group about methods of training and those which were known to be more successful than others. I recall her words now, many years later, as she commented that each time we raise a hand to our companion animals we irreparably damage the bond between us.

I also knew that recent research points out that punishment based methods of training are far less successful than reward based training, and this, happily is reflected in my local training club where I ventured with my current dog, Ollie.

Now my dilemma became a little pressing. I recalled how I repeated the oath with pride, when joining the veterinary community, to uphold the welfare of the animals in my care, and also to 'do no harm.' I felt a proactive step was needed to try and point out the problem involved with smacking a little dog such as Sam, where the human being had to be over ten times his size, or of smacking any dog for that matter. After a long dilemma, I took a training book on my next visit to Sam's home which explained the benefits of training using positive reinforcement rather than corporal punishment.

In this day and age, where we are all sick of the 'big brother' approach towards childcare and other social matters, I was sorely temped to say nothing and forget all about it. My conscience, however, would not allow this to be glossed over, and I decided to risk bringing up the subject. Sam's human had always struck me as a very nice person, and perhaps would later look back and be glad that I spoke up.

I broached the subject, and there was short, stony silence. He took the offered book, and then changed the subject, clearly embarrassed to be having that particular conversation.

We did make a revisit appointment, and he solemnly returned my book after Sam had received his treatment. "I did read it," he said to me, and no more was said on the matter.

It was the first time in a long time that I felt my role as a protector of animal welfare had prompted me to intervene in so personal a matter, but with hindsight, I am very glad that I did.

*　　*　　*

FEELING CONNECTED
A way out of numbness

Franziska Holmes

ealing is a mysterious process, both in people and animals. My training to become a physiotherapist many years ago consisted of following a prescribed route, which had the cause-and-effect theory as its basis. This worked surprisingly well in most cases I saw, but the failures engaged my interest most insistently. There was the question 'why did this treatment fail, when it was successful in all the other cases with the same symptoms?' Individuality came up as the answer and although that had a ring of truth about it, my gut feeling was that there was something else. At the point in my life when my body was showing signs of dis-ease with the daily ignorance of my gut feeling on a practical level I was asked to take part in a clinical study which was looking at the effect of manual lymphatic drainage on horses.

The lymphatic system is part of the circulatory system, together with arteries and veins. Manual lymphatic drainage is a physiotherapy treatment where the lymphatic fluid is mobilised manually to help sluggish flow. Witnessing the staggeringly noticeable impact this light touch modality was having on the treated animals in the most positive way, I decided to sell my flourishing physiotherapy practice in Wales to set up afresh in Gloucestershire in order to be central to horses and went about working with them for the next ten years. I wanted to find out why they responded so much better than people, especially as I was breaking a lot of 'rules' in the cause-and-effect book. I treated them unrestrained and without them even wearing a collar so they could be as free to move and respond to my intervention as naturally as is possible in the confined space of a box.

A few years into this I was joined by a very important working partner, Beatrice, a Doberman/Alsatian cross who had been picked up roaming the city streets of Gloucester. She was four months old when she moved in with me and did not lose any time in escalating my turn-around. She followed me everywhere including the stables where I was treating other people's horses. There I noticed that the dog's behaviour and the response of the horse somehow felt connected; the horses never minded her entering their space after they had completed a greeting ritual which, as I learned over the years, told reams of what was to unfold during the treatment.

By watching the trinity of our responses I witnessed the very subtle reaction of different body systems and again over the years it became clear that those systems were only split into categories for the convenience of verbal communication among people. Not only are our bodies a whole entity, but working as a trio with Beatrice and the animal treated, then later with the herd in a field, I became aware that our responses always followed the pattern of wholeness. At a later stage still I noticed the cows, the llamas, emus or whoever was occupying the field next to my working area were joined with us in whatever was happening. The llamas in particular were very good in picking up emotional change about to happen, which was extremely useful if my working group was made up of ten or more excitable horses with Beatrice and several other dogs in tow!

Apart from the large animals helping me with my discoveries of connectedness, little ones like spiders, flies and mosquitoes were joining in the teaching process. Everyone knows that during summer flies, and in particular horse flies, are never far from where horses are. As my body reacts quite violently to the bite of a horse fly I was particularly wary of them. I discovered over the years that insects like flies settle on areas of the body where there is stasis, i.e. inactive body fluids. If one starts to activate the fluid as in my case via craniosacral therapy or manual lymphatic drainage, the fly, be it horse or otherwise, takes flight. In southern countries like Greece it is the custom to hang up bottles with water to attract the flies and the staler the water the greater is its appeal to the insects. On a similar line lies the appeal of certain plants to the devastating appetite of slugs who are happiest on a compost heap or faecal droppings, in other words decaying matter.

It took me quite a few years to come to the conclusion (having started with the theory that slugs have their place in the interconnectedness) that slugs only attack 'unhappy' or instable plants, e.g. forced, artificially bred, wrong place, wrong soil or even a caretaker who 'ignores' the 'emotional' needs of a plant. By accident rather than design I tested my conclusion through with five tobacco plants, which were given to me in a very healthy looking state by a friend. I, of course very eager to make sure that all five did well, gave them different sunny spots. One plant was demolished within 24 hours by the very efficient slugs that frequent my garden and I later learned that tobacco plants hate the acid soil into which I had put this unfortunate specimen. The second and third lasted a week or two, both in poor soil that needed feeding. The fourth did so well that I left it to it only to find it had gone a few weeks later. The fifth and only surviving plant was positioned just outside my office window in worse soil than two and three and not ideal conditions but it grew into a very strong and fertile plant and I put it down to that it was the only one of the five which had my daily attention.

On another occasion when I had planted a treasured newly purchased plant into ideal soil and spot it got demolished by a fast advancing army of slugs, left for dead as my assessment was, but because my grief was so strong and long that I was not able to dig the plant out for weeks after. I remember crying uncontrollably for ages and when after weeks I felt strong enough to face the dead plant it was showing signs of life, which to my lasting joy were never again touched by my friends the slugs.

My orthodox training in medicine had taught me that as long as I followed certain rules and procedures the desired effect would be achieved; the common rule being the cause and effect theory. This turned out not to be true and what I was learning while I was working with the animals and plants was the theory of chaos changing from the point of quiet centre. In *The Turning Point* Capra (1982) describes how all of the great crises of our times—terrorism, war, pollution, crime, energy, unemployment, health care—are facets of one and the same crisis, a crisis of perception. We are applying concepts of an outdated mechanistic worldview to a reality that is not understandable in those terms. "The mature scientist knows that cause and effect are elusive because of the presence of multiple correlations. No properties are uncorrelated, all are demonstrably inter-linked. And the links are not single chains, but a great number of criss-crossed pathways." (Adolph E F, 1982).

The animals have no problem with that statement.

*   *   *

GOD HAS FUR

I have discovered after all this time
what I always knew.
That God has fur !
Radiant with the fire of a
thousand stars,
God's hands and feet walk the animal way
with fur as soft as thistledown.
How else could the Divine touch
the aching heart with such compassion ?
Or keep vigil on the wounded dying
with dignity and grace ?
Or warm our nakedness with unconditional Love.
I am in no doubt about this - God has fur!

© *Stephanie Sorrell*

PART FOUR

THE WAY FORWARD

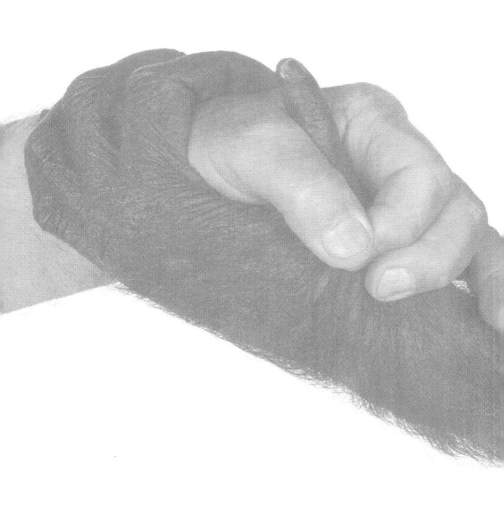

BRIDGING THE ANIMAL/HUMAN DIVIDE

Stephanie Sorrell

*The white man has been only a short time in this country
and knows very little about the animals; we have lived here
thousands of years and were taught long ago by the animals
themselves. The white man writes everything down in a book so
that it will not be forgotten; but our ancestors married animals,
learned all their ways, and passed on this knowledge from one
generation to another.*
—A carrier Indian, from British Columbia
(extract from *Becoming Animal*, by David Abram).

As a writer, I am passionately interested in words, their
origin and how they are used to divide and separate as
we all as unite and animate. Here, I am intrinsically fascinated
by the division and unity which exists between the human and
non-human dynamic, the animal. I understand that 'animal'
comes from '*anima*,' i.e. having breath and soul. So this is life
force, a process of animation. The whole of creation breathes
and is animated, suffused with the Divine.

Looking at the word 'human,' it is made up 2 components:
'hu' has links with humus and the Earth, but—get this!—'*hu*'
is Sanskrit for God and is described as a 'love song' for all

creation. The second component of 'hu-man' is 'man' which originates from 'hand.' So embedded within our unique humanity is the potential to be Godlike by utilising the potential of our hands! We are defined by our hands, our ability to create, manage the environment, the soil, the work place. We talk about 'man-agement' that has its fingers in every pie and is 'hands on.' If we lose our ability to manage and to keep 'in touch' with the situation it spirals out of control and becomes wild and untamed.

I believe that we have a grave responsibility to remove the divisions that separate us from our animal brethren. So how can we bridge this separation between humans and non-human animals?

The first change we can make is in our use of language: i.e. by taking away the 'us and them' dynamic by which we divide and rule. The names we use can extract the vital humanity which is what connects us to our animal nature. In our language we amputate, assign, and divide non-human animals in a variety of ways. I am reminded here of Joan Dunayer's in-depth work on 'speciesist' animal terms in her book Animal Equality. And as author, teacher and activist Les Mitchell writes,

Non humans are never murdered, but culled, processed or harvested. We eat meat or silverside but not flesh, we have on the table a leg of lamb but not a lamb's leg...

As language can stir our deepest feelings through poetry and song it can also anaesthetise the potential to be in right relationship with our animal brethren. Language itself is not the enemy, it is the way we *manage* language that creates the divisions.

War and antagonism are created in the furnace of our own fears and desires. Yet as teacher, White Eagle, says,

> *The animal kingdom is closely interwoven with human and spiritual evolution. This is where danger lies both in breeding and slaughtering animals for man's indulgence. Whilst man permits the slaying of animals, he cannot hope to escape the cruelties and the terrible suffering brought by war and disease.*

This suggests a second level of change. As human animals at the top of the food chain, we wield responsibility and power for better or worse. We worry about environmental issues and yet the hot potato that keeps being passed hurriedly around is the methane generated by intensive farming of livestock. Methane is over 20 times more harmful than carbon and, overall, contributes more to global warming than all the carbon generated by the transport industry worldwide! So why isn't this being addressed more cogently? The hot potato holds because animal parts bind our economy together, literally, in the form of glue, emulsifiers, chocolates , biscuits and shoe leather... and the list goes on. Basically, we are embedded in animals and animals are embedded in us.

The third change is to practise rediscovering and honouring our own innate animal senses. I want to include here several instances where I have been in touch with my own animal senses and I am sure you will have many of your own to share and reflect upon too.

I had a friend in Southfields with whom I used to stay for a long weekend every month when I was studying in London. Travelling down from West Cumbria and then across the London Underground, I was weary when I reached my destination. My friend lived in a long street that seemed to go on and on for ever. I would walk along, breathing in the fresh air, and gradually feel myself drop down into myself. I had reached my destination; now all I had to do was find the house. Usually, I would forget about looking for the house number and simply relax and enjoy the feeling of the ground beneath my feet and the wind cool against my cheeks as I walked, simply trusting my senses to lead me to my friend's house. Then, just when I thought I must have overshot the house, there it would be, hanging in a musky scent as I checked my step. As the pungent foxy scent enveloped me I would recognised the house before me, the curtain, the books in the window. I did this many times over six years. The foxes stayed there, always informing me I had reached my destination, my guiding compass the scent markers they had left in that spot. I was grateful to fox for guiding me 'home.'

Last month, I was staying within 50 yards of a wolf sanctuary in Texas. As always, Mystery, the Alpha wolf would lead the wolves in their 'song' at certain times of the day, usually after feeding time, but at other times as well, especially two o'clock in the morning! I would wake up, hear them serenading the stars and smile, knowing precisely what time it was.

One morning, I was relaxing outside the trailer in a chair

with eyes closed, listening to the wind keening through the trees. It was a gentle fanning through several distinct cadences, a little reminiscent of distant waves on the beach. As I listened I was struck by the familiarity of the sound. Like a record playing somewhere in the background that I had heard at some time in the not far distant past yet couldn't name. I went through the places I had been recently been where there were trees. Siphoning through the memories that were held in my sensory library, I hit blank after blank. But, like some tantalising scent, it wouldn't let go. I tried another tactic: wondering how this murmuring cadence made me feel…It made me feel at home… And then I remembered, it was here that I had first heard the sound, again and again… last year, the year before and before that. I felt at home here… this was my *second* home. My animal senses had known this, held it unconscious, until the light broke through and I sensed I was home.

I believe that our deepest intuitions are embedded within our animal senses. Senses that long to find their way, their voice, in our busy world.

*　　*　　*

THE WOMBAT PRINCIPLE

Marian Van Eyk McCain

The well-known Australian writer and gardening guru Jackie French once explained to a class I was attending the primary principle she had always followed when making her gardening-related decisions. "I never do anything out there," she said to us, "that I cannot justify to a wombat."

Such respect did she have for all the creatures who shared her piece of land that she saw their life together there as a commonweal, a vast co-operative venture in which everyone's needs were met, everyone—from the smallest bacterium to the largest mammal—contributed what they had to offer and everyone thrived.

For many years, one of the members of Jackie's co-operative was a wombat she nicknamed Smudge. In one of her books, she writes:

In those days I was living by myself in the bush—somehow when you live on your own away from other people it's easier to become close to a wild animal. In many ways I think Smudge was the closest friend I have ever had.

And yet...

Wombats are so very, very different from people. Wombats

don't 'see' the world. They smell it...Sometimes I think knowing wombats is as close as I'll ever come to meeting an alien. Wombats are creatures so different from us that it takes decades to understand the way they think and live.

To me, those two comments, put together, sum up everything we have been trying to say in this book. The two comments sound like opposites, and yet they are not. They are like two poles of the same magnet: two sides of the same coin. At first glace they seem to create a paradox. Yet, as with so many other paradoxes, if you spend enough time thinking deeply into this you break through into a new way of seeing the world in which 'either/or' is suddenly transformed into 'both/and.' Yes, it is true that all other life forms are, by definition, different from us and sometimes they seem as different as we imagine aliens from another planet might be. And yes, it is true that at another, deeper level we are all related, all connected, all of us merely leaves and twigs on the same vast tree of life. We are irrevocably separate from all other living beings and at the same time totally connected with them.

I doubt there is anyone among us who has not experienced these same two extremes when it comes to members of our own species, especially those who are nearest and dearest to us: our family members and our friends. There are times when we feel so close to someone that the boundaries between us seem almost to blur and yet at other times, when we suddenly become super-conscious of our differences, we can suddenly find ourselves facing that same loved one across the Grand Canyon. This strange dance, this pulsation of positive and negative poles of relating, is something that is probably familiar to all of us.

Hopefully we have learned that the key to successful relationships with members of our own species and our own families and tribes is to respect our differences and to value them. Dealing with our differences is one of the ways we grow and thrive, and differences are essential to life. Nature thrives on diversity.

Likewise in all our encounters, all our dealings with other animals and all the other forms of life that, like us, are part and parcel of the body of this living planet we call Earth, there is only one principle we need to remember. It is about respect and I think of it as The Wombat Principle.

Our encounters with others, both human and more-than-human may at times bring us joy, excitement, fascination and feelings of love and connectedness. Or they may bring fear, anxiety, repulsion and feelings of strangeness and alienation— or at the very least they may evoke indifference. But whatever the nature of the encounter and whatever the feelings it evokes in us, if we are fully respectful of the other in every way, then all will be well. And if we can all learn to follow the Wombat Principle which is to hold both a loving sense of connectedness *and* a deep respect for difference together in our hearts at all times, all will be right with the world.

*   *   *

I THANK MY ANCESTORS

After Joanna Macy

Thank you, infinitesimally Great
Grandmother Worm, for gifting
us the swirl of blood pulsing
through our bodies to feed each tiny cell;
& praise be upon you!

Thank you, Ancestor Fish
for evolving vertebrae that lend our spines
the flexibility to move, to bend,
to walk upon our feet;
& praise be upon you!

Dear Fish, thanks once more
for bequeathing your jawbones
to become the stirrup/anvil/hammer/eardrum
that allow us to hear other beings;
& praise be upon you!

Thank you, old Cousin Reptile
for a brain that alerts us to danger;
and to you, Paleomammal, for a limbic
system opening us to pleasure;
& praise be upon you both!

Thanks, dear Monkey Sibling,
for developing eyes at the front
of your head! It freed you to climb & leap,
while binocular vision gives us all focal depth;
& praise be upon you!

Sister Ape, thank you for sharing
your DNA & your intelligence;
also for hands to learn the use of tools—
may all beings pick up appropriate technology!
Then praise be upon us too!

© Helen Moore

EDITOR'S NOTE ON LANGUAGE

One of the most effective ways to create change is to start with language. Those of us who have been involved in social movements to eradicate 'isms' like racism, sexism and age-ism have noticed that to challenge habitual language patterns is often to jolt others (and ourselves) into a new awareness of their own perceptions, beliefs and attitudes.

Our culture is only just starting to be aware of another rampant 'ism' and that is 'species-ism.' Just as racism and sexism are defined as the assignment of different values, rights, or special consideration to individuals solely on the basis of their race or gender, speciesism is the assignment of different values, rights, or special consideration to individuals solely on the basis of their species. This is why, as you may have noticed, an effort has been made to avoid speciesist language in this book.

So here, there are no 'pets' and 'owners,' in the relationship between humans and their companion creatures. There is no changing of pronouns from the animate 'who' to the inanimate 'that' when the other referred to is not a human being. And I have adopted David Abram's term 'more-than-human' to refer to those others, rather than the more common term 'non-human,' for the same reason that nowadays we speak of 'single mothers' rather than 'unmarried mothers.' It feels so much more respectful to define them by who they are rather than by who they are not.

Speciesism, like those other isms, can lurk very deeply hidden, both in our language and in our psyches. Such is the lifelong conditioning to which we are all subject. So if I have missed any lurking speciesism in my own writing or in my editing of this book, please accept my humble apologies.

—Marian Van Eyk McCain

ABOUT THE CONTRIBUTORS AND FURTHER RESOURCES

ABOUT THE CONTRIBUTORS

David Abram is a cultural ecologist and environmental philosopher who lectures and teaches widely on several continents. Named by the Utne Reader as one of one hundred visionaries transforming the world, he is a Director of the Alliance for Wild Ethics and the author of *The Spell of the Sensuous* (Vintage Books, 1997) and *Becoming Animal* (Pantheon, 2010). He is also an accomplished storyteller and a sleight-of-hand magician and has lived and traded magic with indigenous medicine persons in Asia and the Americas.

Clea Danaan is the international, award winning author of green spirituality titles such as Sacred Land, Voices of the Earth, and Zen and the Art of Raising Chickens: The Way of Hen. She gardens, homeschools, and writes from Colorado, USA.

Franziska Holmes, who died in 2006, was a Chartered Physiotherapist who qualified in Germany and worked in hospitals before going into private practice, eventually including animals in her work, which evolved to craniosacral physiotherapy. She taught at postgraduate level for over 15 years and was a past chairman of the Craniosacral Therapy Association of Chartered Physiotherapists and also a member of the Association of Chartered Physiotherapists in Energy Medicine.

Helen Moore is an ecopoet, Forest Schools practitioner and community artist/activist based in Somerset. Her debut collection, *Hedge Fund, And Other Living Margins*, was published in 2012 by Shearsman Books.

Eleanor O'Hanlon has a degree in German and French language and literature from Trinity College, Dublin. She was a communications co-ordinator for Greenpeace International, and her work took to remote parts of the Russian Arctic. She left Greenpeace for another leading environmental group—the Environmental Investigation Agency, known for groundbreaking, undercover investigations into the illegal trade in endangered species, such as the trade in elephant ivory. She was featured as on-screen investigator in the award-winning ITV/Discovery Channel series Animal Detectives, which exposed the illegal trade in wildlife around the world.

As a writer, Eleanor has collaborated with some of the world's outstanding photographers of wildlife and wilderness. Her articles on wildlife and conservation have appeared in magazines such as BBC Wildlife in the UK, Animan in France and Switzerland, Nature's Best in the US as well as live webcasts bringing together nature photographers and writers for the protection of wilderness. *Eyes of the Wild* (Earth Books, 2012) is her first book.

Kathleen Martin is a retired university professor and a developing gourd artist. She loves the world of ideas, her tools, hiking in beautiful places, and growing things. She is a grandmother of three, mother of two sons, partnered to a wonderful man for many years, and a never-too-old environmental activist. She shares a photojournal blog with three wonderful forever-friends.

Marian Van Eyk McCain is a retired psychologist and the author of seven books. She edited the anthology *GreenSpirit: Path to a New Consciousness* (Earth Books, 2010) and is also co-editor of the GreenSpirit Magazine, a free-lance writer, book reviewer, columnist and blogger.

Sky McCain is an American citizen living in the south-west of England. He likes walking, playing the trombone in his local brass band, and visiting his favourite parts of southern Europe. He has also been involved in 'green' activism in the local community and was the founder of the Wholesome Food Association, an organization that champions local food. Sky graduated with a BA in History from Boston College in the US and has an MA in Values in the Environment from Lancaster University, UK. He has had a lifetime interest in religion and spirituality, starting with Christianity and continuing with Buddhism and Advaita Vedanta. He has recently focused his attention on Gaia Theory, climate change, and the relationship between science and spirituality.

Susan Meeker-Lowry is a writer, herbalist and organic gardener. She is the author of *Economics as if the Earth Really Mattered* (1988) and *Invested in the Common Good* (1995)— both from New Society Publishers—and numerous articles. She lives in Maine, USA, where for many years she published a newsletter, 'Gaian Voices: Earth Spirit, Earth Action, Earth Stories.' Currently, Susan makes herbal body care products which she sells through her home-based business, Gaia's Garden Herbals.

Dr Rupert Sheldrake is a biologist and author of more than 75 technical papers and several books, his most recent books being *The Science Delusion* (*Science Set Free* in the USA) published by Coronet in 2012 and a new, 2013 edition of The Sense of Being Stared At which was originally published by Arrow in 2004. He is a Fellow of the Institute of Noetic Sciences and visiting Professor of Holistic Science at the Wisdom University, both in California, and is the Perrott-Warrick Research Scholar, funded by Trinity College, Cambridge. He lives in London.

Stephanie Sorrell lives in West Cumbria where she writes and works as a clinical support worker in a local hospital. She has an MA in Psychosynthesis Psychology. Her latest book *The Therapist's Cat* is, on one level, an amusing and romantic fictional story, but on another level holds moral undertones of how our mistreatment of animals can impact on us at a later date.

Suzannah Stacey is a veterinary surgeon (a member of the Royal College of Veterinary Surgeons) and a qualified veterinary acupuncturist. Even after treating animals with acupuncture for many years it never ceases to surprise her just how profound an effect this type of treatment can have on a patient's quality of life. She feels that she will always be learning about this subject for there is an endless amount to learn and such a lot that animals can teach us.

Susan offers veterinary acupuncture in all species; the majority of patients being dogs or horses. She is careful to minimise her charges, as she feels it is a treatment that should be open to all. To make this possible she uses other vets' or therapists' premises for her appointments, or does home visits if this would suit the patient more. And since she lives simply, she is happy to charge just what is necessary to cover her bills. Suzannah may be reached at the Veterinary Acupuncture Referral Centre in West Sussex.

Hilary Wilmshurst first found affinity with some of 'All Our Relations' while growing up in the wonderful wildness of rural Dumfriesshire; on holiday, also, on the Northumbrian coast where she exulted in bumpy, battered-taxi rides across the sands to Lindisfarne (pre-causeway), and boat trips to the Farne Islands. She has been guided by the gifts of her power animals throughout a life of teaching, counselling, mentoring and parenting—a life enriched for many years by support, challenge and development in a peer Transpersonal Learning Community. She now lives on the N. Yorkshire coast which inspires her to walk, photograph and pen a poem or two where, amongst others, porpoises and peregrines people her world.

*　　*　　*

FURTHER RESOURCES

For details of all the contributors to this book and links to their website, plus information about other titles in this series and where to get them, please go to:

www.greenspirit.org.uk

*   *   *

GreenSpirit
magazine

GreenSpirit magazine, which is free for members, is published in both print and electronic form three times a year. Each issue includes essential topics connected with Earth-based spirituality.

Find out more at www.greenspirit.org.uk

"For many of us, it's the spirit running through that limitless span of green organisations and ideas that anchors all the work we do. And 'GreenSpirit' is an invaluable source of insight, information and inspiration."
– JONATHON PORRITT.

GreenSpirit
Path to a New Consciousness
Edited by Marian Van Eyk McCain

Only by bringing our thinking back into balance with feeling, intuition and awareness and by grounding ourselves in a sense of the sacred in all things can we achieve a new level of consciousness.

Green spirituality is the key to a new, twenty-first century consciousness. And here is the most comprehensive book ever written on green spirituality.

Published by Earth Books
ISBN 978-1-84694-290-7
282 pages

Meditations with Thomas Berry
With additional material by
Brian Swimme
Selected by June Raymond

Selected and arranged by June Raymond, especially for GreenSpirit Books, this is a collection of profound and inspiring quotations from one of the most important voices of our times, the late Thomas Berry, author, geologian, cultural historian and lover of the Earth.

Published by GreenSpirit
ISBN 978-0-9552157-4-2
111 pages

GREENSPIRIT BOOK SERIES

I hope you have enjoyed reading this little book as much as I have enjoyed editing it, and that it has whetted your appetite to read more in this series and discover the many and varied ways in which green spirituality can be expressed in every single aspect of our lives and culture.

You may also wish to visit our website, which has a resources section, members area, information about GreenSpirit's annual events, book reviews and much more: **www.greenspirit.org.uk**

* * *

Other titles in the GreenSpirit book series

What is Green Spirituality?
Edited by Marian Van Eyk McCain

The Universe Story in Science and Myth
Greg Morter and Niamh Brennan

Rivers of Green Wisdom: Exploring Christian and Yogic Earth Centred Spirituality
Santoshan (Stephen Wollaston)

Pathways of Green Wisdom: Discovering Earth Centred Teachings in Spiritual and Religious Traditions
Edited by Santoshan (Stephen Wollaston)

Deep Green Living
Edited by Marian Van Eyk McCain

The Rising Water Project: Real Stories of Flooding, Real Stories of Downshifting
Compiled by Ian Mowll

Dark Nights of the Green Soul: From Darkness to New Horizons
Edited by Ian Mowll and Santoshan (Stephen Wollaston)

Awakening to Earth-Centred Consciousness: Selection from GreenSpirit Magazine
Edited by Ian Mowll and Santoshan (Stephen Wollaston)

More details on GreenSpirit's website

47771133R00068

Printed in Poland
by Amazon Fulfillment
Poland Sp. z o.o., Wrocław